the seven-eight count
of unstoppable sadness

the seven-eight count
of unstoppable sadness

Marcella Polain

PUNCHER & WATTMANN

First published in 2023
Published by Puncher and Wattmann
PO Box 279
Waratah NSW 2298

https://www.puncherandwattmann.com
web@puncherandwattmann.com

ISBN   9781922571540

Cover design by Shaun Salmon
Cover image by Marcella Polain
Typesetting by Morgan Arnett
Printed by Lightning Source International

NATIONAL
LIBRARY
OF AUSTRALIA

A catalogue record for this work is available from the National Library of Australia

to my family

that we must be very strong
and love each other
in order to go on living

Audre Lorde, 'Equinox'

Contents

four

five

six

one

alive

1
at last the sky bloodied
behind the ghost gums
an exaltation of birds and
fat thoughts that
splat my edges

2
my brother is here for new year our
mother thinks he's balding from
poor nutrition I laugh she
watches teenagers massing in the
beachfront carpark is delighted doesn't
see the bottles a woman kisses the
restaurant window my brother waves and
smiles a man falls over his friends
roll him into recovery position the
maitre d' calls an ambulance some
where glass smashes we pay
the bill guide mum to the
car the police turn up red
and blue she says *what*
a beautiful night
I never saw so many
people promenade it
makes me feel alive

3

the road north is narrow straight
beside a thin straight train track
and on both sides short thin trees
beyond, the country becomes flat grey-green
two poets in a car a hundred ks an hour
from the train track a black cat crosses
just ahead running full stretch

eggs from nests

1
who stands howling
flings open my eyes
sets the dog to snarl
strips skins from trees
and eggs from nests?

at breakfast the world
barely breathes

2
once she had wanted to drink lovers with
wounds deep enough
once she had a different name
wrote neat and desperate
to them and her mother
for love
mercy
sliced oranges till every surface ran
then
lifted them to her mouth

I wake to knowing

the room is cold   deep   still as a pool
night stares back: a wet open submerged face
hair and clothes stream into
a current of dreams it
breaks the surface of   to gasp

today all day I'm remembering and walking all wrong ways

yesterday I laughed telling you how I
closed the front door on a woman as she blessed me a
pamphlet about souls fluttering like breath inside her hand
you blinked
mouthed a sound not quite laughter

time baffles   still I've been young
my brother a clown knife-sharp a
stiletto and me the shrieking sideline laughter
if you crack the crown of my lightly boiled
head the smaller me still swims the white of
my brain waiting to be the shiny centre

I am wounds I forget then remember then forget and
this body will never turn pointed turn funny turn scalpel

still my mouth insists   spits
stories laughter breaks bewilders
closes doors and the faces of
beloveds turns like nights and
days and nights insisting into

dreams to wake in that
blue pool of knowledge:
drowned woman turning to
wards me slowly from inside
her own current her black
eyes two cold holes peer
into mine her long hair
being swallowed by
the contents of
her mouth

return of light

cat curls in a corner of chair
heater breathes across the floor its
exhalation passes through window
folds into dusk how can anyone

be sure which way she
turns her face to the pane
closes her eyes because it's
still not night and time
makes living vertiginous
longer than she imagines even
cats have to roll themselves into plugs to

she thinks *if I stay here till morning*
that would be all right there
are people for whom daylight is just
horizon glow for days and days so

later then later she opens her eyes to see
a sky can be less purple than a room
watches night thicken into soup and still
she doesn't move

cat wakes becomes
a statue of itself

fall blink

all afternoon a fan chops thick air
I dream an empty house have
dreamt this house before in all its
woodenness but sometimes it's a different house

from the back door the yard is dust   discarded things
I look down   each time I blink the
ground unfolds   becomes a flooding pit
underfoot foundations crack and drop
the house teeters
I blink again and something breaks the
water's surface – boulders or a giant's spine – and
from the falling yard brooms and balls and buckets topple in

then beside me suddenly a clutch of children
I flap my magic wings like hands to shoo them safe behind me
and there we are at dream's end   I am fixed:
stand guard; now never sleep (or wake)
our small ones mustn't slip into a
silence; no single moment's
startle
       under
          blink

road

moon yellow as a tipped cup above
the tree-line   flat black road its
white edge holds us in its slender and
relentless grip

pale verge-posts   their reflectors wink red as
roo's eyes and sometimes tail lights curve and
dip and rise as if over the hill is a future and
not the swallow of road as

if road is melody to thread through us
the soft black wash of this night forest its
improvised trees uncertain as smudges uncertain as
those roos in our shocked white headlights and

we don't mention the hairs inside their
illuminated ears in the moment they turn to face us or
the pale underneath of the owl that swoops
did did you see that white thing jeezus that
and the next bend twists the chill on the back and
I just
I just want
I just want to stop

agape

1

songs enter my hands from the sweet wet green
my bone-cold mud-caked fingers sing
cross-legged   alone as a child
again plucking weeds
sucking their stems
only a breath between me

2

if I could only touch your
face   companionable chest of
drawers   oaky grain of you
at once symmetrical surprising
elegant as a river
one white pill and I'd lie
still more would drift me in
your current past the desk the
fire-place erupting joy
from the chimney

3

we leave the window wide and
night rain flings itself in
by morning the sky's slashed
blue   the wind's off the
sea and the air is
white with plumtree petals

in ones and twos they circle and
close in   clean as the souls
of children   their small wings
cling and flutter   toward
inhalation

duplicate heart

night is cold
there is no wind
walking home I
scoop a stone slip
it in my pocket
stand on the corner
a lone car passes

light greens I
walk again slide my
hands into my coat
to the talisman

a voice from behind
crystallises the stillness
hair rises on my neck and
my heart makes a duplicate
drops it into the well my gut's become

time is a hole too I've stepped
through   I look ahead
the street shudders itself in
to a new hard shape   the car
dinal points   the
city skyline   the
distance between me and
home blade-sharp so close

he is
walking closing
I look at my gate
if I throw the stone I could hit
I grip   hold still   my ground my
breath   to turn
to face   to hold
hold

boiling jam at christmas

this year it's spring up to christmas and daily jacarandas burst
I stand surprised along the fence-line between us and the abandoned house:
our plum trees are still burdened their slim arms bowed by the weight of fruit
above the blue is split by a white screech of cockatoos
at my feet the long grass rustles
I tumble scores of purple plums into my skirt take to others with a spade
walk home slowly my belly rolling

under incandescent light I prepare the sink
inspect each one bathe them all
pat them dry   lay them on the steel bench
the firm are packed into the body of our fridge
the soft and broken set aside
over the greased preserving pan I press two fingers into
them flick out their stony hearts
make a red flesh heap
my jam boils fast and thick
my hands run red red red and I clean everything
set out the jars snip lengths of silver ribbon circles of gold paper
I do not think of the abandoned house the rustling fence-line
or the night-garden busy with its shallow graves

on the first sign of illness she:

is a dawn glimpse in the bathroom mirror
everything she knows about herself is
held quiet in the flatness of its palm;

is dreaming of the life she steps away
from as unknowingly as   smiling
she might step through a door or
into a car or from a kerb;

is at work immersed in the words she writes
the page she tries to grab between her
thumb and forefinger;

is the shot of pain elbow to wrist
is her pincer grip springing open
is the page floating to the floor
the sound of it skidding;

is driving a small tan car –
a small tan car is all she has –
and is also the small tan car and
the pedestrian stepping out elsewhere;

is the speeding road also flat and blank;

is road (static) and car (travelling);

is the marks she makes (on board page car road)
the mirror she collects with the palm of her hand
that she doesn't understand but
holds and holds up in the hope she'll
see what blindsides her and what
her life will be now that she

is end-over-ending her small tan car/body
every shot of its strange blue pain
all the other faces in the work-room swivelling
towards that peg of her thumb and finger involuntarily sprung
and the sound of the paper's skid as she
steps into the path of her own collision

infusions

plastic tubing snakes its yellowness from
a hanging bag to hand

beside a man who must drop his trousers
to rearrange his underwear and colostomy bag

the ward is overbooked
someone doesn't joke about a growth industry

once set up in the small square staff room
only the fridge speaks and intermittently

the sink is stacked with dirty dishes
over it hangs a large oil in a wide gold frame

there's a storm at sea

on hearing of the death of maggi phillips

of course it's not possible
birth's sheer physics and
yet we fill our pockets –
twigs and stones
questions hope –
until bulging
it's us that burst from
this bright and fleeting

impossible
each of us a universe
with one hand weaving our fabric from
memory and dreams and forgetory and
with the other unravelling our weft

that we don't even realise
how the days spin on:
punnets of tomatoes an irritation dinner
fingers tap across a keyboard afternoon

two

beneath

'But you must always realise the truth of your original face'
Ben Ming, *Daughters of Emptiness*

this morning the sea holds its colour like milk
and from its boulders stream strands of vivid algae
a determined wind from the east
the sky full of bruises

walk the high tide line seaward
sand firm damp and cool underfoot

eventually a seal will rise from the milky-green suspension of the sea
you will know it by its glistening brown head that
turns to look about and
by the way it doesn't see you
the way it slips beneath and vanishes

splinter

everywhere lies the open face of earth and rain falls on this face
all that has ever been taken returns and everywhere earth slips its skin
so much rain the arms of earth no longer hold
so much that rain fills nose and mouth covers the body of earth

we build higher
watch the geometry of rivers shift
bus stops stairwells offices
land vanishes   pond lake river sea all water
becomes just water just pressure at the windows below us
our foundations below them
we cling   feel our buildings shudder the way forests shudder before
    the blade the
way sun shudders horizons   the way glass and
bones like light splinter

trees

1
open each morning fill
the sky with longing
who will become the pitch and cadence
the seven-eight count of unstoppable sadness?
we are torrential   our
voices open soil   dig
holes for ourselves   and
any seeds we hold are washed away
we cling to all solutions to drowning
a leaner life   winter-bare   our
skeleton holding its bars as if
waking tomorrow depends

2
if trees were trees only
would names fall from them in
such abundance

if we were only selves
we'd detach and leaf through air and light
landing softly elsewhere

crabbing

along the shore spark pinprick lanterns
in the silty shallows our toes cling
water pleats about our knees
our torches shoot their beams
odd angles refract
illuminate the nocturnal sub-marine
glimpse other ways of being or
bounce back into our uplit faces
our fists hold timber poles worn smooth
that dip our nets

then snatch
lift into air   legs
clatter onto   backs and
legs   and
tumble into the open
mouths of buckets

then this

everyone says the kitten is deaf that
soon she'll be flattened   or
worse, come home dragging her broken
self   that she should have been
drowned   would have been kinder   but

I watch the way she watches the
way she stretches whiteness over
white floor tiles flicks her tail
and calls   calls as if I'm deaf
as if there's nothing more than this
moment this
body this
scratch
then

emergency

1

april air cold and gold   grows older
cat turns herself inside out
furniture shivers   I'm alert as a chair
for sirens   for words
for something I don't yet understand:

yesterday   summer tailed into easter sunday
an electric blue yellow beach morning when
something wide translucent red floated in
on the skin of the sea

strangers gathered   ankle-deep
to greet this unfamiliar   then silent
watched it blacken sea foam
rush the shore

surfers paddled south
parents called in children

2

this oil-creature slipped
from future and past slipped
from our western horizon
warning   consequence
devastation   visitation

broke into hundreds of thousands of bubbles
that popped and dissolved and sank into sand

all afternoon I rolled bits of beach between my fingers
thought how omens blindside
and   like love
rearrange the heart
leave no evidence for
the naked eye

3
when you and I snap our silence in two
I will say:
run   darling   if it means you'll live
run mornings evenings afternoons then
stop turn
run again

if you wish to
run from me
I will say:
there is nothing I won't and no part
I push my hand down my throat
scoop out my heart
it appears for you here

I will say:
if you wish
run toward me
every door is flung
for your escape
I wait   it's cold
if it means you will live
take aim

scatter

in a clearing a handful of seashells
baked hard in sand

a hawk wings against the sun
its shadow cuts

a pale scatter of rabbits
the earth itself

three

for bird and all who love her

set a ring of lamps

if our lives were cinema you'd
die in a sweep of snowy winter we'd
drag the kitchen table over ice-burned lawn
we'd gather stones to jam beneath the table's feet
lay you out cold and sumptuous among some
leafless trees and hard-pruned roses with
your favourite hat and books   some speckled eggs we'd
bash the frozen earth with forks or fists then
set a ring of lamps round you

when night's bitterness sets in we'll
watch from the deep-set windows for foxes   watch
the fire in the range   watch
for you to stir   watch
the clock's arms twist till they shred its face and turn
that time to snow that falls insistent and
buries us all but
winter isn't fiction where we live

we prepare nothing are prepared for nothing and
not knowing what else to do   can return only
to love   love you harder as if
ferocity will forge the question we can't
will crack the carapace that holds your true self from us
reveal you as profound and ordinary as us all
so we can tell you: nothing exists, lovely girl, that does not also hold its remedy
and this includes despair

the day you die is warm and
still you die you die and
if there is another place then there you are
still with your smirk but without (I hope) the knowledge of
the ferocity   the insufficiency   of our love

bird poems

1 bird lemons

the house next door will not stop weeping
fat lemons rot on the tree cats leap in the grass
you would fall down laughing at their spring up the wall
their mouths full of legs like grey furry fangs

we moved here just ten days after and I
stared at a neighbour in his baggy grey shorts beside him a
woman studied the ground slowly I raised both open hands and
he blinked at me as if he knew
every morning that summer we opened our eyes and couldn't believe it
each dusk we saw him shift his sprinklers heard him mutter *where's*
    that baby gone?
then in autumn a car door opened and swallowed them whole
now suits with clipboards sometimes chatter on their porch

come back bird I keep making jam
you could have traded with them: a jar for lemons
you could have promised them a soft sweet pie
listen bird can it be spring again?

2 bird magic

warm rain saturday night
we walk the damp park beneath hissing trees
punters smoke laugh all wear black
the doorman's eyes flash his smirk
he stamps a small grim reaper on the whites of our wrists
inside young men stare but
your mother and I watch only for you
there and there: those are your legs shifting your weight then
dancing wild at the front your
short satin skirt beating the air your
beret sweating and pale on your head your
mother's fingers tight around my arm

sunday in the shower I stare at my wrist
the smudge of death weary on its staff
the same bruise-purple as the last dress your mother bought you
how she washed and dried and held each part of you and
afterwards bird you should have seen the magic she had made
your lips shone almost as if you could breathe

3 bird turning

bird it's june again   I walk home against spinning clouds:
in a garden bed furious with roses a cat laid out flat
its staring eye its fuchsia collar its fur the colour of chimney smoke
the tiny gold bell at its throat

the crowded afternoon bus stop   a lull in traffic
buses and cars idling at the lights stare at us from up the road
two boys step out in their blue school shorts their white shirts their faces
    shouting:
who wants to play the death game the magic game?

later I stop at an intersection   think about where to buy cake
a silver car filled with laughing boys hurries against the amber light
a woman and her daughter in a four-wheel-drive
begin turning

4 bird intermittent

magpie flutters to my feet
tilts the sculpture of its head its beak black marble soft
stares and polishes the light in the jarrah of its eye
I smile back   it circles   its claws click on stones   its
throat pulses glossy black and plump
behind me it pauses   looks at sky
when I turn again it's vanished

sometimes I think I have become rain or you have
that people peer at us   that we threaten
are intermittent   that
whatever we plan we evaporate   that
everything we fall on catches or absorbs us

at dusk I step out   it's here again silent smiling

5 bird another kind

a favourite photo and
of course it would have been your idea   commanding
all four of you up the jacaranda to scowl down at me
the wide black lens in my hands   the slow way it winks
I intruded   my city yard is small   my city life tame and
where to release all your wink and terror
don't smile you would have told them
you all so artful perched one per limb (and
that's no accident either) to gaze
past my fences to the playground the well-behaved park the
pond and its reedy island its
nesting ducks and the cars flapping endlessly down the highway

once I was also girl and clambered up things and leapt

where you lived forests abut verandas
houses tuck under   coiled as in tales
where you lived you'd slip the boundary in a breath into hills gullies creeks
in the kitchen your mother made everyone food   watched through the
window for you but

what of the other days   of you just grown   alone   all doors ajar each
wardrobe open   trees leaning at every window   and you room to room
     turning
over plans turning in your hands the imagined slip and leap of how to

no – I want another kind of ordinary: you opening the front door to do
     nothing but
listen to how other creatures – frogs birds trees snakes – live   how they
     come

close with their green and shining eyes   how you step back smiling to let them in

6 bird blossom

bird last year your mother dug our garden with her fingers
searched for something she couldn't reach –
order beauty reason –
found a sting that wounded sharp invisible
that sent her reeling across the face of the world
a smiling top her bright metallic arms outstretched
in china she piled stones to hold back rivers
worked all day and night to hold back tears
in chile she dug tunnels deep as fault lines
hooked her fingers into miners' beards
yanked them bawling from their graves
on the arctic rim she crawled up glaciers
leaned across volcanic maw and spat and
her spit froze there as it fell sharp as diamond and as black
bird all this she did in memory of you her
legs grew thick as trees and her eyes rattled

7 now bird

the day is just this line of windsurfers
their hurtle and skip converse
their stalls are them gathering
themselves

above gannets stall too and
clear sighted turn their
bodies into spears   fall
vanish re-appear wings filling
beaks with fish thrashing while
behind them falling
water shatters

today a poet said no-one should write about birds anymore

I said nothing
your name in my mouth like a stone

bird   the wing of memory is unbidden and
makes unkempt its shapes swoops and calls
it settles and regards me
permits my gaze if
I am still but
what else is a body except
movement? it flies I
follow to gather shells and
feathers and find myself here where

sun and breeze are fierce
all sails hard-filled and
gannets vanish   resurface
where along the sand gulls settle
into hollows to wait out the rest of the day

a woman dives into the face of a wave and is gone
light glitters where she's been
in a moment she will re-appear
hair streaming

8 bird fuchsias

oh here you come knocking again
wondering where they've all gone
oh I have to – I need – oh
bird your mother flew as far east as –
flew vexed   her arms cut
loose   and dropped to
earth by
a creek   and

into a house so neglected she
spent weeks cleaning but – well
you know her spells – now
her garden keeps its eye on her clip
clip clip the giant fuchsias
wheelbarrows of wormy straw

a duck mutters in the shade of her carport
butterflies hold sunlight in the cup of their wings
she watches from the veranda
orange cat asleep on her
images of you inside on her walls above her sink by her bed

alongside her driveway   in thick reeds by the creek
snakes press their bodies to listen

9 bird prayer

sleepless between dark and light and
dark find forgotten boxes full
of tins that rattle in the hand then
lift each lid to reveal a peg

on a palm a
peg can be a caught body
in tin it sounds like bones or drums or
incantation

last time I saw you as you left
your cheek was clammy cold
I touched your forehead
with the back of my hand the
way women identify ailing and
looked into you seeing
your body held the panic of the
world and all its promise but
you locked out my gaze and nodded
small closed speechless as
if you'd just been shaken

now sleepless to release prayer
for hours of every dark and light

release prayer
lift every lid and
look a much longer time
hold more closely
to release prayer keep watch

10 bird rectangle

1

where we live most sheds are
sheets of steel perfectly rippled the
way the wind ripples dunes in time and light
the practiced eye can estimate by glancing
at the shape of shadows just how late it really is

2

where we live walls and floors are rectangles
as are bedheads and windows the tops of desks
keyboards and screens but
most keys are square
(square being a special rectangle)

3

where we live vacuum cleaner hose is tubular
detachable from the body of its machine
for flexibility
(sometimes these hoses are also rippled)

4

where we live most cars are built on rectangular principles
including windows so
lowering one splits that principle in two:
glass; no glass

viewed from the correct angle
the ignition slot's a slender rectangle
(a sheet of note paper, however, remains a rectangle
even if it will always be blank)

5

where you live/d a child who has never known the world without you in it
alights from the bus and after
the sound of the bus has faded
the sound of another engine puzzles him and
he lifts the shed's roller door
(rippled it rolls up shrinks inside its own mechanism)

6

where we live the casserole dish in my hands is round
full and shrouded in tea towels and
passed to your mother as if it contains what we seek

later the child will stare into it the way he stares into his hands
someone will knock the table's edge as they stand
water will ripple in its glass

7

who will open the kitchen drawer
to see the roll of tape you used to
fix the hose to the exhaust
neatly returned
to its place

11 bird horizontal

the wind's ice hard south
you should see its glare behind the olive trees
blue antarctica

some time after you bird I begin to speak:
generation to generation, bad happens, builds
my daughter completes my sentence: *and then crushes someone*
I should have known – and I do
but knowledge needs time to become itself
needs tucking away to take out today on this hill
staring into the storm through the grey-green
leaves blown back to front and flat as a horizon

12 bird stop

1
there's something about the tone of
half an avocado sliced face-down
spread as a fan across
a royal blue glaze
about the inside-out of cucumber and
its white wet glistening seeds
about the honeyed satin wood of
your mother's table beneath my fingers
that stops my breath

2
and just inside your
father's door a
twinkling mannequin:
your tulle
sequin-scattered
party dress

four

to my brother richard

I step from the car and you are the
djidi djidi bird   small brave and
at me from the shrivelling prunus leaves

my first confidante and playmate
my better   my sometimes nemesis   you
arrived so early – feet-first a bloody torrent –
nuns held vigil for days beside you and our mother

continents apart now for more than half our lives
your voice through the phone to me is always twenty
and I'm opening my front door to you asleep on
my morning porch after you'd pitched up drunk that
midnight and didn't want to bother me and

still every conversation turns   returns
to coming home – for years your adamant refrain

you have left a self here
I have kept it safe all these years

I can never truly thank you for being a sixteen-year-old boy
on that morning getting in the car for school;
for being the one who saw me slip by – the one our mother had
kicked out   who needed clothes;
for re-entering the house;
finding me cowering – believing the footfalls were hers; and
for bending down to kiss my cheek
see ya, you said
yeah, I replied, see ya

visiting you (lantau island)

1 first night

wake to a
cry curling into my ear
from a neighbouring high
rise through my small win
dow then once
again wake mouth op
ening breathe
can't breathe
believe the ringing alarm the
not knowing where the
world a catastrophe of green
as if jungles have slid from mountain
sides pouring greenly into the cups of

2 from the sixth floor

beyond the living room window mist floats
jungle mountains loom recede
all day sea becomes sky becomes sea
I peer past treetops and into its density
listen for your return your voice on the stair

– a flash of wing
birdsong pierces

to an imagined sister

1
neither the full story nor figment you are
twenty-seven letters nine syllables
from our mother's mouth a
dum di di dum di di di dum dum line
to skip to in the sun   skip to
when the sun is skipping in my
face when everything is just
the scrape scrape of soles on stones as
if something were stuck there singing:
I had a miscarriage at six months
...a miscarriage at six months

you have never been a face in the
luminous you-shaped air never twisted
from dreams like a cork to appear as a
version of yourself by the end of my
bed   nails scratching your own shoulders your
wing buds' feathers wetly split
startling me awake
never hovered
descended theatrical or tapped
my melancholy window

2
beyond the pane
the rag of sky turns
birds shout like optimists
light licks my white walls

whiter   dust
spins the
cat wails the
road gorges traffic

a first morning thought:
you grew where I had just grown and
it was me bawling and hungry
refusing our mother's breast trying to
tell her you were there
and she bawling too

3

upon waking there's remnant
scent   sometimes sweet and breadly
made   sometimes sooty as burnt paper
and the instincts of breathing be
come acts of survival be
come acts of remember:
you were here
you   in the world
thin   fully formed
eyelids fused as buds

there's a mouse in my bedroom wall, sister
it scratches loud but I know it's
the size of my thumb

4

not one photo of our mother pregnant but
here is my first birthday:
her belly deflated as if you'd not just

she's closed her face
practising
perhaps
the compression into
only seven words
our father watches
someone else and
no-one sees the strange
error of light that later develops:
a smudge like a burden
laid at their feet

5
more and more it seems
possible I miss you
memory and imagination
beaks excavating wormly strange

more and more   poems are
creatures hungry   half-wild
circling and   circled
each morning woken closer to and
closer and which
(like you)
I know will
never love me back

bus tree

footpath moves under my shoes and socks   the bow of a blue
hair ribbon bobs by my eye   look across the intersection everything
is wrong is shock is the bus already there but shouldn't be shouldn't
and this white and blue dress this favourite dress its sound its rustle
on arms and legs walk fast then faster then fright then run the bus
already there but what's the time it's never there I am the bus already
starts   its loud and louder everything is just its motor but it's
never its motor till I'm sitting on it run run it's already motor it starts
to move and run run run blue hair ribbon favourite dress it already
moves it's slowly slowly down the hill and run and run it's turning the
corner and run run and I'm still here what's the time near school on
the wrong side of the on the wrong side of everything should have been
over there waiting at the bus stop by the lolly shop that's a tiny house
made of wood all alone in a big empty block of long grass and crickets
and sunshine calling to one another a tiny house with a door and a bell
that tinkles when it opens so the man knows that I'm there if I have an
extra halfpenny and the bus isn't there yet but now right now it's already
turning already turning running its back to me calling and moving away
from me waving

along the school boundary a line of giant eucalypts
I watch the bus shrink and hush and vanish over the brow of the hill
listen till it's really gone   look ahead
the lolly shop is completely still   look down
gravel is gravel under my shoes and
on it the shifting of light and shade   look up
at the ends of long limbs leaves in fists are shaking themselves   look down
ants climb the ochre pebbles   look behind
strips of bark hang from the trunks of trees   look up

bird squawk
inside my shoes
toes curl and clutch
know how to anchor to the safety of earth
ahead sunlight spread all over the road

haunting

all men have been traces   their
knees your knees   their
fingernails shoes cigarettes keys
you call me in their voices

how long will your death stab
rob voice and breath
leave part of me alone and begging
just to help you grill cheese on toast
just for your ghost

all days have been your last –   your
strike that sent me across the room   your
kiss to the top of our mother's head   your
tyres on the gravel –
even the happy when I run
lift my face to sky I know is only sky
not curtain blue bowl screen
when I don't watch – there; no
there – for a glimpse of you

how much life it's taken dim-witted me
to see why you will never come
to see I've done the haunting

each bloom's throat

1

and that tree again
symmetrical and bare last
week now its red tongues singing
over blue's morning sky I
cover my ears I
cover my ears

2

mama today you'd be ninety
I will lunch alone imagine
I have wheeled you to this table by the
window imagine you too see the rainbow
lorikeets alight twist and hang – purple yellow
green as feathered figs – for the sweet in the
base of each bloom's throat and

3

you are delighted and I hear you
last night as I dreamed
you spied an empty corner
crept into my mourning head with
your blankets stories your precious
things and I awoke my bones shuddering
into another august the red curve of your
kiss your birthday smile your
vivid laughter bursting

wink of the sea

this high-rise night is a windy cliff
beyond the horizon a crescent of beach where you
bait   cast   where the deep tugs the glinting
line in your fist   reels in the
smile of the moon glossy as
a slice of honeydew
your face is every window's face your
eye the wink of the sea and you
are the gleaming scales of the fish I slide from my bed to
catch moon-juice gilding edges

rain comes and goes or comes and stays
and goes when you least expect
this is the coldest winter I can remember everything wet
hail wordless and urgent
the tin of our roof our window-glass   even the cat
leaps from the walls
every part of my body hurts   I have become the
rattle of a walnut shell a thread of seaweed   I
scuttle across the night-time floor open and close my limbs
like scissors
I wake the neighbours
christ if I can't
ever hold your
hand again

flat out love

so I lick the moon and what does it give but
age and bone and long long longing to
sleep and and and if you want a flat out love a
love like paper for your ink I'm not even close
not as thick as a plot or a belly
not as thick as a fat red sun and
lick at you just look at you green and
fresh as a plant new-picked and the
sky curving over like a soundtrack
your voice high as a needle
as a note that arrives from far away
a note I've stopped reaching for
you're a screech a scratch
you're sticky subcutaneous
you're simultaneous de
partures you're a sin
gle destination and if
you want a love like a
flat out page a belly and
some ink come close my
one and only stamp and
let me lick you

shore of the dissolving perfect

1 gap

your name in my diary:
five letters large enough to fill the day

when we meet there may be three of us
your face will fit the curve of my throat
I will make tea and sit over here
you will sit by the door perhaps with a child in your arms

again again your laughter will disarticulate
me and when we wave goodbye I'll jangle
my arm each joint undone and mid
afternoon will stagger to bed

but if
if tonight I woke to your voice at my door
whispering my name through the gap
I would spring the locks light the lamp
and let your mouth dismember me

2 a clean jar

there are moments – I could have stoppered this
put it away in the back of the cupboard
I line up those moments like sweets on my sheet each beautiful
and lost:
the handshake the bus the letter the glance

what has happened should have remained a thought
now what specimens are we?
we moulder in the dark pickle in juice from a two-
headed creature
we are a briny invisible stew
we are fishers we are melon men of rain and scream
drifting seaweed threads deep blue cliff enormous no-eyed creature-fish
we're scissor fins to cut our hands to cut the lines to cut the tongue the
glinting moon to cut us off cut everyone

now I need a jar to hold the entire mess of the sea

3 stopperfinger

our houses float on the thick surface of sleep
we stand by its lake and my finger touches yours
I breathe in slowly   out slowly   in slowly out
blood hammers my head
no-one knows you're here no-one knows where I am
you resemble the perfect sleeping husband I the perfect sleeping wife

we stand side-by-side on the shore of sleep
our sleeping breathing sounds like water
my finger touches yours and leaps
we are watchful mute under all the mute and watchful trees
the shadows of their arms are on us
our houses float my finger's touch and leap our

breathing feet are sleeping wet at the edge
my finger leaps the lake's thick surface our   thick wideness
shadows touch   blood hammers our houses where
the husband sleeping the perfect wife
my finger slides into my mouth and
I am mute   you watch me while

we're shadow breathing in both our houses made of
sleeping
every surface sounds like water your breath floats
my mouth is seeping
I'm your watcher your stopperfinger
blood leaps mute and side-by-side
you are the wet and sleeping lake I am standing close
and my blood leaps and hammers you

we slide and seep into our sleeping houses
we resemble we reassemble ourselves watchful husband
watchful wife
wet our fingers   dip and open   breath through stoppered
hammered mouths we're thick as shadows   trees side-by-side
we're lake and blood and arms and leap

4 click

what must remain:
my eyes blank as a consonant; my smile a small new apple
he wants to hold its greenness smiling
back at my smiling smile everything aglow
night-time terms have become uncertain
something has fallen away but when?
I scrabble about on the floor; I cannot find it

nor allow any vowels between us they are as round as my hips
I dress myself before bed like a widow in the hope he will not recognise me
I click my tongue; he understands I have become an exoskeleton
if he clicks back there is nothing to do but fall insect-silent insect-still
all eyes closed all limbs pressed together in prayer

5 forgetory

a fish of a thought leaps at me from the bathroom mirror
time twists and shivers; I stare
at the moment before you shook my hand
already it was all too late
back here I hold on   imagination speeds
ahead decades and
everything inside me falls

what will remain of this?
not even longing and a late confession
not even a secret slipped into death's fist
once you said *I have a memory and I have a forgetory*
each day re-arrange myself
ascend the morning deck
think my lines before
I speak of anything
god my head is tender and
shouting full

6 smoke

bus speeds us over bridges
night falls   city draws near   buildings elbow sky
river blackens to silk   all the office lights   street lamps
quiver the surface white and gold
pale water birds trail legs like lines of smoke

your wrist pulses beside my wrist
I stare into the long white flesh of your arm:
a brand livid pink
you tug down your sleeve
I turn to the open window
rows of boats safely moored stare back

some views of love

to MW

1 even then

1

the cat's claw you spot
in the upholstery and
lift to the light to study

your face turns
intent as a nib
concentrated as ink

2

even at three am when the cat sleepless
wanders our room keening as if
we have abandoned her (as
she always knew we would)
you rise softly from bed
to enfold her

3

outside our night window
the horizon a glitter of ships

morning we stand on a white smile of sand
though there is barely sun you dive as always
grinning   your legs frantic at their hidden work to
shout *how lucky are we? look where our parents landed us!*

2 the long way

girls like me take the long way home
build futures from other
lives through windows:
a lamp woman at a table
one abandoned shoe a squeal
clock kitchen sink one
gleaming fork a
laugh an open
pair of scissors

these days our own rooms are full of
sun of air shaped by songs we sing
you across the table the
scratch of your pen –
lists stories crosswords poems –
your chin thoughtful in your other hand

these are unlikely years we've made
single days when you have turned
your key have called my name your
footfall in the hall the wheels of your
bicycle humming and curved
as the neck of a horse

some days that girl looks as if she's
here and smiling back at you but
there is something that tells you:
wait; she's walking slowly and alone

and so you watch for her then
tip your hat and bow   your
smile vast as summer

3 limpet

night slides cold into our
and morning wakes us old
we cling limb to limpet limb
our mouths agape: oh
look at our eyes four
grey holes in our
paper skins our
spines break we
crack open

4 cloud stutter

between our sheets
skin hair spit
shaken from love or fever

our hearts like clouds
stutter

5 the art of divining water

side by side on the escarpment over
our city the wide snake of river
souwesterly steals our
words in its rush of
air and light
from below
orchestras of traffic endlessly tune

you say *the art of divining water is not
in the rod but the hands* not
the bones or muscles but
the blood drawn to its
wet familiar deep
in the damp sub
terranean

you say *we are a tic in the eye of time*
it has never flowed like river has
always held us closed over us
its soft fist
I say *look* one finger pointing *the way sun stabs the river's skin*
all around us trees continue birds
yell their wings rising you
take my hand your
fingers trem
bling and
damp

the missing you

1

tonight I feel you further from me than tomorrow
eyes hurt can't sleep get up start walking though it will
take years to reach you the years pass anyway like
a continent underfoot   each sole gripping
releasing repeating repeat   but it's also
true that I understand nothing except that
once I cradled you and now you're so far
out of reach and daily something fizzes
under my skin long and slow and electric

I hope you're asleep and dreaming horses
I've been writing of dreaming horses and
remembering the years of nights sleep fled
from you left nothing for us to do but wail
remembering the muzzles of horses soft
and their breath sweet and you
have earned your horse dream flight I've
been writing your hands in their manes
your fingers twitching

2

five-year-old boy on one chair in a row of chairs
is wearing a red jumper
we see him from the back
once you had a red jumper
it's your colour and we've
all been small and we've

all worn jumpers and in
every place children have
red jumpers

four-year-old boy another chair another country
just stares ahead
we see him from the front
his world is dust and silence and
he's dust and silence too
blood gaudy on his head
he swipes at it
gazes at the red on his hand as if
he can't understand which of course he can't

we can't see the five-year-old's face but we can tell things from behind
his arms pulled up the way we truss dead birds for cooking
handcuffs above his elbows because they've not been made for the wrists
    of a child
and maybe that's the mercy because
I think the world's much too big and
I will take too long to reach you and
being a child is a terrible thing

what a name means

1
from the veranda we watch livid rain
and after of course it can't be true that
nothing moves though that's how it appears
every leaf shocked

how long have we stood here?

like time the air is skinless
we can see a clear half mile to
the valley's other side:
the sharp-edged tread of a tractor tyre
its hub a red wound
leans against a rippled
shed green as water and
beyond   a home – bricks
pale as beach sand
an orange skip bin in the yard

afternoon continues
under the setting sun the orange metal
flares   blooms tangerine as
a flame till it burns

2
somewhere upstream there's still rain
beneath the footbridge the river
roils a thick brown tea and
above its air is only the ecstatic

voice of water

lean against the railing
listen   watch
feel the world shudder

3

the marri six storeys high are not themselves
each windward branch recoils
from the bared teeth of weather
each spray of leaves shakes so
hard that we shake too
each leaf dagger-shaped and
knifing the brilliant afternoon

4

what is time and distance if not perspective?
that tallest marri isn't fooling anyone by
sprouting green from the scorch of
its trunk that travels all the way to
its crown nude and grey as a twist of bone
and up there – thirty meters from earth –
a raven perches staring south to where storms come
I watch its balanced concentration
raven knows what raven is but
cannot know what a name means
we watch wind buffet its feathers into the gleam
of fathoms of deep blue ice

5

in the car one summer I pressed play the
tape hissed blasted *beds are burning*

so loud through me that you flailed like garret so
I smiled watched my belly undulate
brown as sand and imagined you

the morning was bright and hot and
I was young alight momentarily alone
sending my brimming body's love to you –
such joy awaits – and believed I was
watching you dance

forgive me

6
it lay on the doorstep neat as a gift
my heart rose leaned to one side
rattled then leaned the other way
the yellow flash on its
flank bright as a gash
its crown feathers wet
as if just born
it could have fitted the curve of my hand
and though I didn't yet know why
I thought of you and of

a time long before we met when I ran
every day building time and distance
which I now know are identical
and even then I knew you   knew I
was running all those years towards you
drawn the way light is drawn

the way it draws its own path
as it makes the sky

nothing

(after Audre Lorde)

you   knock
I   unlock
throw my arms
about you
cry and don't
let   do not
let go

what's wrong you say
while I breathe your
living body

this day strikes
a bell
strikes true
here are words
least valued
women's words
like: I adore you
like: how I miss and
          am heart sore

so I step back
gaze up at you
rest my palm against
your confused face the
way I did as I birthed you
love you now as

fierce as then
as fierce as
all the days
and nights
of your silence

say nothing

five

attempting incognito in western armenia (istanbul 2015)

of course he breaks the first rule:
follows a spruiker down some stairs of wide white stone
I follow (woman alone on the street unthinkable)
together we descend

behind a low partition a surprised tanner butts his cigarette with
one hand retrieves his hammer with the other and smashes it against
his work bench   shouts as he reaches for another skin
I turn away   step so close to a rack of coats and
belts that open and then close around   surround me that
I must step back then
lay my hands on trembling shelves of leather boots
it's hard to think   hard not to think that everything here has
      once been

he sidles up
through a high window we glimpse the stairs rising whitely to
the street   and people's passing feet and
still it's hard to
hard not to –
let's go I say –
think what's happened here
how people   like animals   just disappear

a hill road

ravines either side
no tree a
bare shoulder our
car pulls up on   ticks   cools
its body open and us
emerging unfolding into
the dusk the breeze all the way from
massis[1] presses sky
snow-melt cold

follow down deep into litter of stones
down until all above us loom boulders
ruined air   a wreck of cloud
heads down we trace bend un
pick earth's seam
something has erupted here:
obsidian mounds – glittering as knives sharp and
black as satan's fingernails – slice our palms   pockets

night drops   our feet clamber slip
our names   echo stone to
stone   wind their way up up and
back to the empty car

---

[1] Armenian name for Mount Ararat, symbol of Armenia, currently situated in
  Turkey

we sit silent in its belly
the road to yerevan² is endless
the black bag knocks and rattles in the boot
the headlights point ahead always ahead
who else sees our tongues lick the blood from our hands
tastes the metal at its core

² Capital of Armenia

diaspora

if I could map
you would be each
name a pearl a loop of
more than one hundred
years each knit a
thought-string thin as
light's skin fine as
spacetime in its curve
twist stretch to meet
this point this pen this
pin I hold to prick to un
pick some of history's blisters

what leaks but fluid time?
try memory
try love

if I could unmap
you would be land
be language   gods
be lives undone each
blood each skin
cell shed each scab
each crusted sore an
island in an archipelago in
all the archipelagos that genocide
makes to keep our wounds from
public weeping keep them safe to

gether out of sight their edges eroding bit
by bit to fall in other nation's seas

how tender new flesh is
how certain and how purpose
ful the heart that studies truth
fulness of oceans' currents the
heart that endless thinks it makes
and remakes shapes of continents

armenia april 2015

a bus lumbers up road blasted from face of
mountain   winds higher tighter colder
as it rises and in case like the world we
forget why we're here or the golden
soporific sun-slant through our
windows   we will recall the
seconds it takes to screech
to stop for a skewbald colt
the seconds it takes him
wild and whinnying as a
ghost to leap from tree
s clenched into rock on
the slope above and
appear stumble and
stagger and pull hi
mself upright to g
lare with the terri
fied whites of his
eyes then gath
er his limbs an
d leap on do
wn the oth
er side int
o mount
ain for
est an
d tur
n in
to

tre
es
like
the
dead

on the death of levon ananyan*

1 perth

all day sky hangs over us exhausted
in evening's fade it strains   can't contain and
rain belts and belts our heads the world awash
we raise our sodden selves to ask:
what will become of all our plans now
that all levon convinced us of is mud?

2 dubai

somewhere between the airport giftshop and
check-in desk past the rows of squat toilets
and bottled water in the furthest corner of the building
someone sidles up and severs my tongue
I have no language: no armenian words ever
so what kind of armenian does that make me
and now no english either surrounded for
the first time by strangers who look like me
my mother brothers sons   look at their
watches phones   not even glance
as long as I am silent and
I am

it was painless unexpected
not bloodless there is plenty blood
always been the blood thumping
in my head   my eyes
restless and wide as stones

3 yerevan

on the first day of autumn –
Levon Ananyan was taken to hospital.
After an hour, he passed away –
must be mistranslated must mean
he's asleep after hard weeks of sun
beating white weeks of
breathing summer's dust he's
tired (of course) armenians are
tired (of course) after more than a
century of walking out of deserts but
still we don't sleep – one ear like
a door kept open for the knife and
one eye for the gun because
nightmares break all locks (of course) and
run around screaming and screening and re
screening themselves and nights are just wake and
wake and wake again to this

we stare at the floor our hands
turned useless as paws in our laps
we beat and beat our heads with them

get up levon get up

*Levon Ananyan was an arts administrator, event organiser, publisher, and
tireless supporter of the arts in Armenia and internationally.

eyes: three

madrid

from the air brown and yellow hills   miles of dry she hadn't imagined
on the ground fat olives in bowls fat cobblestones in streets narrow
    doorways
labyrinthine bookshops slender glasses of beer a blue blue sky the
    shadows their
cool geometry a refuge   swirls of summer people – white skirts brown
    arms
cameras and big teeth flash – trees so greenly bright they hurt the eye

bunbury

her feet in the white sea foam the wind onshore howling her hair from
    her shoulders
her clothes from her skin her every thought from her – and there they
    go flying
astonished up into dusk and only one thought glances down at her in a
    moment's
remembering the body which formed it a warm body and an upturned
    face fast
receding a mouth still smiling at the sky those eyes still closed

trigg beach

aunts watchful and plump in their fold up chairs are blue-eyed and
    endlessly jolly
their husbands a circle around the barbeque not looking at one another
    are talking
sport commiserating in the small shouts of their laughter

one version of arriving in england

through the train window
fields fold themselves into
water meadows blinding as
lens flash

sometimes black and white cows
look up surprised they are
hinged at the ankles to their
puddled double soft

cloud gazes down upon the
mirror of itself *here traveller* they offer
you want a bath you want
a pillow to rest your head on

after the station then a villa
ge's cobbled streets are also
rails to drive her on her
suitcase in the hitch of her hand

she has become forward movement
headache a shut mouth
keeps a wail coiled in her throat

upon china

moving through shanghai as if it's real
as if it's whole   organic
as if you and me and the taxi with
its glowing lantern of meter

in the window the spectres of
lantau mountains flicker   I turn to
look at them but they vanish
and who can blame them
even in the dark my eyes can see:
it's flat here flat shanghai is flat
its once abundant delta now
miles of industry of dark factories and
even darker towers where
factory workers live and dream –
who can blame them – and
I remind myself that everything is meaningful and
flatness means easy roads speed lines of sight

moving through shanghai as if it exists as
if the days I spend there are useful
as if the students I speak to are grateful
as if they don't whisper that they want me to
help them they want me to help them get out
as if I've entered a set in which those
on foot who cross streets against lights are questioned
on bicycles at intersections when front wheels breach lines
are questioned
disembarking their bicycles improperly at red lights are questioned

who walk footpaths, wait for trains, play music in cars are questioned
who make books are vanished (books also vanish)
who tell the world of these vanishings are vanished
who resist argue are angry or distressed – and
who can blame them – are vanished

back home people ask so I say: no insects birds sky few trees
I say: many uniformed and plain-clothed
and I am corrected: architecture infrastructure governance results

a sailor's letter home
(after the old gaol, albany, western australia)

sun or rain they herd us out and mother I am grateful
though our prison walls bare their teeth
great shards of green glass mortared in
we walk round and round inside its upturned open mouth
and I look up for lightning bird or blue but
today I am jarred: grey clouds lid me in

along the walls' base where stone meets earth
rise the small wets of weeds – thistle dandelion sour-sop –
unfurling leaves one by one the green some days unbearable
around and round I pass them   shadow and light
drop upon us inch by inch all the way from heaven

I pass return and in my thumb and finger's nip
catch a living stem crush twist don't break stride
I simply roll it hold it in my sleeve and
oh its scent is wild and bitter

later in the fetid dark I close my eyes and tuck it in my cheek
there all night it melts and I am running running home to summer

mother the world is vast the horizon a lip it must seem
I have sailed over

look up
raise your hand

six

for my saturday writing sisters

repeat/unfurl

behind his head
shelves of books
shout his name at her

                    a blink of thought:

maybe one day mine

he:
smiles *sit*
she:
balances herself her bag   tries
to explain   watches
him watching her   watches
him worry at his shirt
button   loses
her sentences   sees
his button de   tach
him looking at   his baffled fingers

thinks she hears
maybe you can sew this thing   blinks
at all the round things hanging –
eyes button dipthong silence

he:
sets the button on his desk
sets his hand beside it
asks her to repeat

115

low ceiling low lights lecturers and
selected students talk books
she sips cider   stands on a square of
grass called 'the garden' that smells of men and beer
someone mentions a name   says *from last year*
and *she has a baby now*; *imagine*
she imagines   sips
lecturer snorts *that's the end of her*
she looks around but no-one looks back
their heads blossoms nodding on their necks as
if he's opened a door to let in the breeze

she:
wakes from dreaming she has met herself weeping
turns the kitchen tap   water glints   shouts
catches it in a glass moon-blue
pours it down her pipe of throat
her feet squeak along the lino

below windows is street in the-hour-of-nothing-moves-
but-thoughts: that hawthorne story's indelible letter and
when she feels something pull her flesh – the way
years later children will pull apart what she thought
love was – feels her toes butt the floor till the timber
cracks
          feels her body taking root   she doesn't look down
because who would believe   she looks only ahead
one hand round the water glass   the other round
the window ledge   doesn't even believe
herself   her heart high-knocking so that
she:

raises her chin
unhinges her jaw
unfurls her tongue
wraps herself in
brimming red

through creative writing class window #1

as the pen hits it first appears as birds on the law building
four storeys up in their
cobweb nests knitted to glass   mistaking
reflections of trees for the trees   mistaking
glass perhaps for bark   knowing such things are possible here
then one becomes a twisting fish being
netted and dragged up   and then the story lands in my lap:

in the summers when no-one's here everything drowns
the swamp this city represses   leaks into
sewers drainage ponds ornamental lakes replica wetlands
rises up   reinstates itself and twentyfold
sends the suburb fleeing mosquitoes breeding sharks cruising
over all the buildings submerged and then
just as quickly recedes
rushes away to hide
like film reversed

it stinks for weeks

it isn't reported but
there's no hiding that
twisting fish up there

through creative writing class window #2

student-hands work like can-openers
they ask and ask
peel me back
they frown and laugh and
lift their pens   want everything
let them

I want cloistering   that
clear luminous place to sit to
mend with my own pen and
paper clean as skin

the hand that edges over pages
sounds like feet through sand ssshhh a
writer's life is sit and sit but
it isn't: ssshhh
listen to the ssshhh
sibilance of all those bodies moving

an agitated wing (after peter blake's *self portrait with badges*)

your jeans rolled and
it's no love song though
what makes us smile is
not your cuffs or your face or wrist
not the curve of your fingers
nor your other hand hidden
or the light on your lip or the
fence behind with its mess of
green shadow and would
never be your badges or
the red slash of shirt a
vertical wound at your throat

it could be the feather of your shoe
blurred as an agitated wing that
despite your ice blue stare or because of it
even in this performance you can't tame

wild bees

on the third evening I run out of language
my hand leaves only its damp emboss
upon the page
I stare dead ahead through the window
wild bees   blueblack in the failing light
dart in and out of the hole in the
living trunk of the eucalypt
last of the foragers dogged at bottle
brush rosemary lavender

the air is burred by cicadas   the
low sun licks the stalks of grass to
gold   smudges the boulder's curve
dips the scattering of stones
I am empty but the poised world is promising and warm
is growing shadows a mosquito a fragment of lace at the glass
a breeze that hesitates then flees headlong as a spirit through this gully

behind it presses its ghost-print its second stillness: silence then
a honeyeater's trill a raven falling though a minor key a wattlebird and parrot
I am fixed to my chair and slow as glass

what we do

in a shopping centre car park
a driver steps from his taxi he is
folded stiff as an origami bird
daily paper crushed beneath one arm:
my heart steps towards him
thinks *too old to still be working*
then *perhaps only a decade ahead of me*

once nimble as the jack
he doesn't see me thinking we become what we do
doesn't see me at all but a woman catches
my eye and smiles steps aside for me and
my stick and the train of words I drag behind
me cursive as the office chair lounge and
kitchen chairs as words carved from my skeleton that
grind and crack and twist their way out

prerequisites for admission to a writing room

1

I am nar[1]
I will plant a world tree[2] in your garden
I am not invisible
my fury forces rain to fall
address me correctly

2

no locks
no people
real names of all creatures
lapis lazuli and
loved books only

3

I retreat without speaking
I venture out without speaking
I descend
I return each dawn with stories
a bowl of golden apples
at night the scent of grapefruit blossom

---

[1] native Armenian goddess of water, sea and rain

[2] in Armenian myth, an enormous tree which: supports the heavens; connects
heavens, Earth and the underworld; is the source of ancient wisdom

catch

she strikes a match cups that
incandescent citrus world and
the set of her palm her mouth
are orange and full

she leans to kindling to put the flame
hair falling like a wing and glances
through her feathers and she is its
bright and its sharp is
the golden parts of her
fold and the parts of her
glitter

see her lemony spark
enter the red of her
hair and catch

winter at short beach

beside a stove one poet
draws her needle through
repeating stitches
line on line

a second balances
note books   pen
curls the comma of her
body to her lap hears her
writing's scratchy breath hears
waves exhaling in the bay

a third opens the stove door
reads shapes of flame and wood

no-one speaks

Acknowledgements

a hill road – earlier version published in *Westerly* 60:1. 07/2016

a sailor's letter home (after the old gaol, albany, western australia) – earlier version published in *Conversations with ghosts*. Marcella Polain and Paul Uhlmann. 2014. fold editions: ECU, Mt Lawley

bird poems 1-3, 6, 8 – earlier versions published in *Perihelion (online) 2009*

boiling jam at christmas – earlier version published in *Zeitschrift für Australienstudien*: Nummer 22/23 2009. University of Klagenfurt, Austria

each bloom's throat – earlier version published in *My mother: poetry anthology*, Malak Sahioni Soufi (ed). Vision Libros. 2016: Damasco, Siria

flat out love – published in *Cuttlefish: Western Australian poets*, Roland Leach (ed). Sunline. 2023: Cottesloe, Western Australia

the art of divining water – earlier version published in *Oír ese río. Antologio poetica de los cinco continents*. 2018. Echarper, Argentina; Colegio José Max Léon, Colombia

My love and gratitude to dear family, friends and Saturday writing sisters – Elizabeth Lewis, Sari Smith, Jan Teagle-Kapetas, Morgan Yasbincek – without whose support and patience these poems and this book would not exist.

Heartfelt thanks to: Morgan Yasbincek for insightful, joyful editing; to Shaun Salmon for cover design; and to David Musgrave, Morgan Arnett and all at Puncher and Wattmann.